First published 2015

Amberley Publishing
The Hill, Stroud
Gloucestershire, GL5 4EP

www.amberley-books.com

British Library Cataloguing in Publication Data.
A catalogue record for this book is available from the British Library.

ISBN 978 1 4456 4597 1 (paperback)
ISBN 978 1 4456 4603 9 (ebook)

Typesetting and Origination by Amberley Publishing.
Printed in the UK.

Contents

Apres-vous.

Introduction

Whether gleefully celebrating a Wimbledon victory or morosely enduring another early exit at the football World Cup, we British take our sport very seriously, and Heath Robinson is no exception. In this volume, packed with his customary inventions, the beloved artist examines our relationship with sports and games.

Although we all love a bit of sport, it is clear that many of us are somewhat lacking in talent or application; not to worry, as Heath Robinson is on the case. Be it stabilisers for ice skates, body braces for those difficult golfing shots or crowd-calming measures for rowdy games of bridge, the irrepressible artist has solutions for every sporting ill. He also offers perhaps the first recorded example of tetherball!

As you flip through the book, then, reflect on the great pioneers of sport. They did not achieve fame by simply following rules, but by inventing their own rules, treading their own paths through the wilderness of sweaty locker-rooms and snowy mountains in their bids to make the sporting history that we cherish today. So pick up your clubs, squeeze into your swimwear and strap on your skis; there are mountains to climb, oceans to swim and innumerable clumps of grass for your golf ball to hide behind.

1
Good Exercise

Another washout. How to train at home for this year's Channel swim, affording additional proof that England is a nation of sea dogs.

Learning to swim.

Lessons by post: the new Heath Robinson swimming post which is acquiring such popularity at our most fashionable resorts.

Swimming the Channel: some simple devices to ensure success.

For lung power and for the encouragement of elasticity in waiters.

For strength of arm and for power of resistance.

For family transport.

For endurance, and a startling result of over-training.

The enthusiast: a short course of training for the rugger novice.

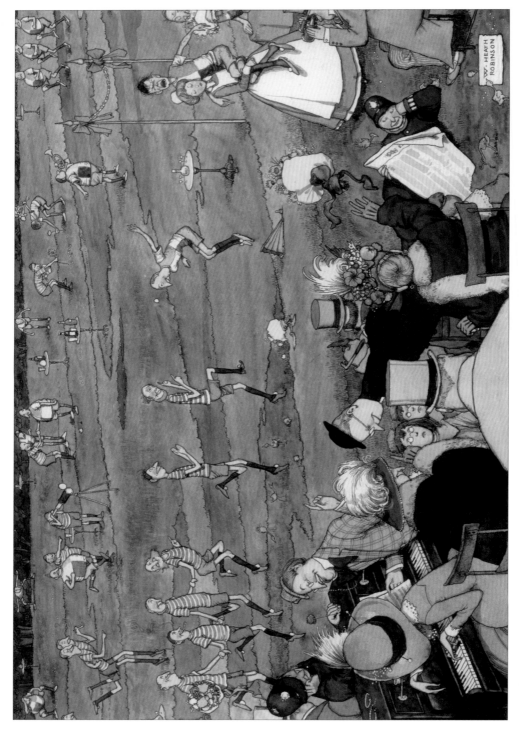

A gentle game of rugby in the botanical gardens.

More rugger trials. A line-out of Mr (Black) Heath Robinson's sketchbook which leaves us quite unconverted.

A remarkable instance of quick skating – a gentleman leaves his shadow behind.

Safety skating.

'It's an ill wind …' Native Swiss profiting by the misfortunes of an eminent skier.

Wild and woolly. A few trot-skis in Switzerland.

Off to the ski picnic.

Self-propelled skating gadget.

A bit of frost: a simple device for making your own snow as you go along.

Ups-a-daisy! A sensible provision now made on some of the nursery slopes, whereby the plump skier may, with the minimum of effort, regain his or her feet after a fall.

The only way out of an awkward predicament.

A new winter sport – the luge glider.

A little pride before a fall. Remarkable presence of mind of one ski-ist called forth by the carelessness of a companion.

2
Bat, Club and Ball

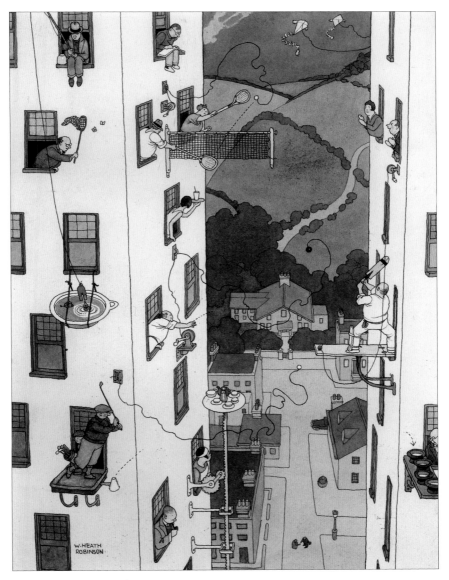

Sports without broad acres.

The fall of man.

Aquatic golf I.

Aquatic golf II.

Aquatic golf III.

THE TEE

HEATH ROBINSON

Aquatic golf IV.

A hefty slice. The tragedy of the too-vigorous putt.

A striking example. The sort of thing that convinces one of the necessity of lightning conductors on golf courses.

W. HEATH ROBINSON.

GOLF BRACES—
FOR FACILE MOVEMENTS

THE NEW OUTFIT—FOR
DISPENSING WITH CADDIES

THE NEW
PUTTING TROWSERS—FOR
BENDING OVER THE GREEN

Some golfing novelties for the next season I.

Some golfing novelties for the next season II.

Down to bedrock: an intelligent method of overcoming a difficult problem.

We can quite believe it. A portrait of the artist driving off the first tee.

How coal was first discovered in Scotland.

Improved golf clubs.

Strange things that don't often happen at golf.

A very cross word puzzle. 'Across: A forceful exclamation!'

Far-fetched. A lesson in unnatural history. The kind caddie-bird of St Andrews pursuing its daily round.

'Here comes the bogey man.' How you can detect the good golfer from the ordinary man in the street.

Annual 'Get-There-First' golfing competition takes place as usual at Tooting Bec.

The incurable golfer does a short hole-in-one.

A parting shot. An unfortunate backhander at St Andrews.

A top-notcher! One of the silly mistakes one makes when it snows in Scotland.

The lie: one of those golfing stories which you are bound not to believe if you don't want to.

Casablanca of the links! – 'Whence all but he had fled!' A modern tragedy of our missing links, featuring a boy of the bulldog breed.

Wimbledon serving tube.

Playtime at Wimbledon. The new craze of jazz tennis caught in full swing by our extra-special artist.

Putting them on their metal. The new tennis practice for cultivating a vigorous style.

'How's that?' Clock cricket – a new and exciting summer game for the seaside.

How it is done: completing a cricket bat handle in the winding grounds of a bat factory.

Quick cricket. A new method of giving both sides a chance of getting in an innings when playing one-day matches.

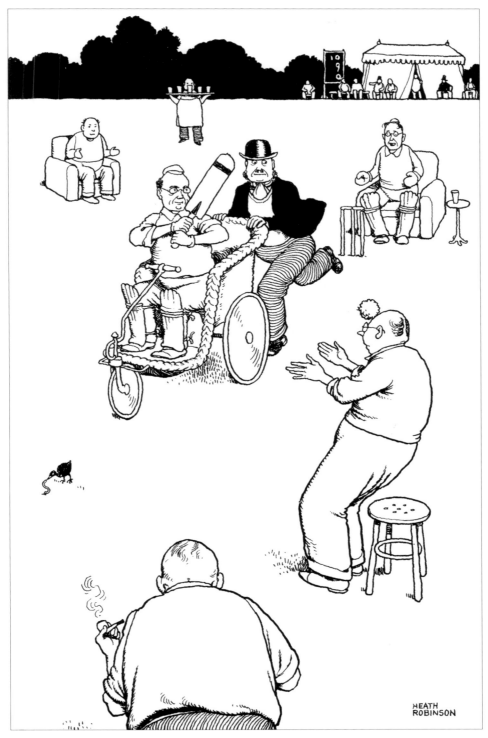

Cricket for the middle-aged.

Potty: how our artist imagines that test cricketers secretly train in order to avoid being caught in any part of the field.

Multi-tennis.

'Hey, "Willow" Waley-O!' Some ingenious suggestions for giving the bowler a better chance. We understand, on Mr Heath Robinson's authority, that they are to be considered by the MCC as alternatives to the new regulations for smaller cricket bats.

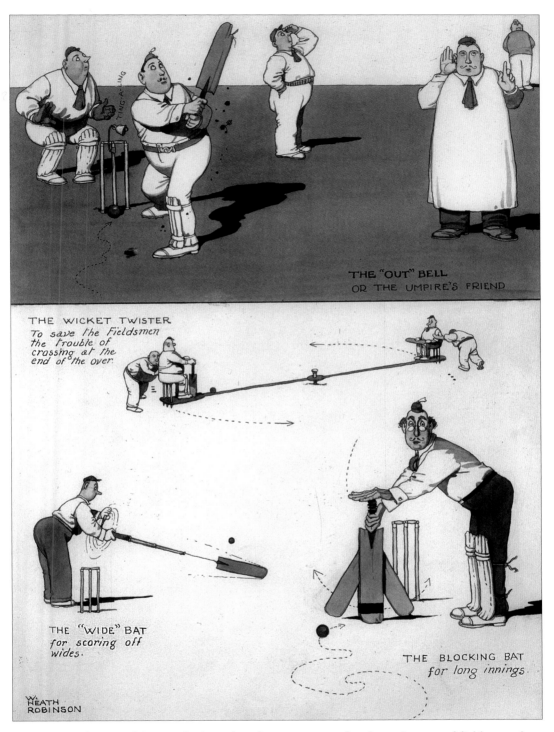

Some cricket novelties – to be introduced next season – for the assistance of fielders and batsmen.

Cricket: Eton vs Harrow at Lords.

Silly points: how cricket is played in mountainous regions.

3
Other Sporting Endeavours

The new winter service. Devotees of rug-tennis, the new game which enables rugby players to avoid getting stale at half-time, demonstrating their skill.

Sedentary sports – lawn tennis for the middle-aged.

Round in one: testing the bias of bowls at a well-known sports factory.

New combination game.

Tortoise coursing: a pastime for the peacefully disposed.

AN EXCITING GAME OF MIDGET FOOTBALL

A THRILL IN A GAME OF MIDGET BASE-BALL

A HAPPY DAY ON THE MIDGET
TENNIS COURTS AT WIMBLEDON

MIDGET POLO PROVIDES
EXCITEMENT WITHOUT
DANGER

Midget games.

Foot golf.

Six-handed draughts.

Monte Carlo reformed – playing snap for filberts.

Cue-ball – a new indoor game combining the subtlety of billiards and the vigour of football.

The new gambling dance.

'It takes two to make a quarrel.' How to smooth over those little differences that sometimes occur in bridge.

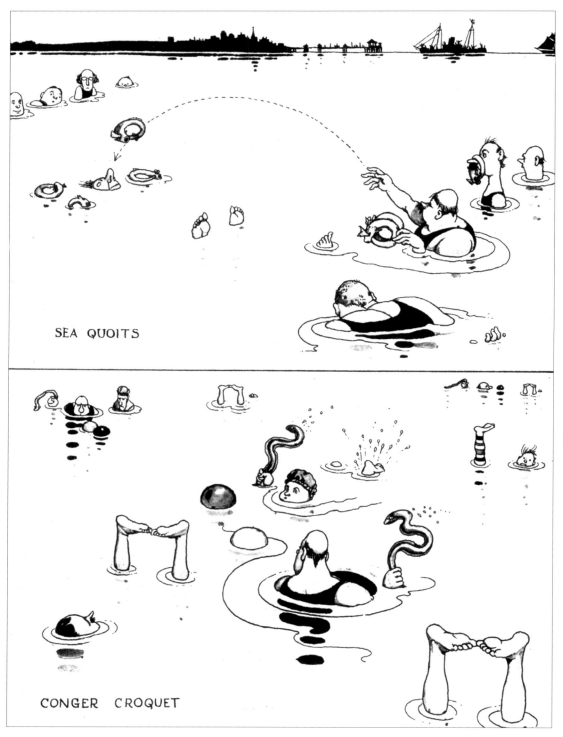

SEA QUOITS

CONGER CROQUET

'Heath-letics.' More new water sports for the holidays.

Training polo ponies.

Spearing wild moth in the Canaries.

Birdnesting in the Adirondacks.

Snaring eaglets in the Highlands.

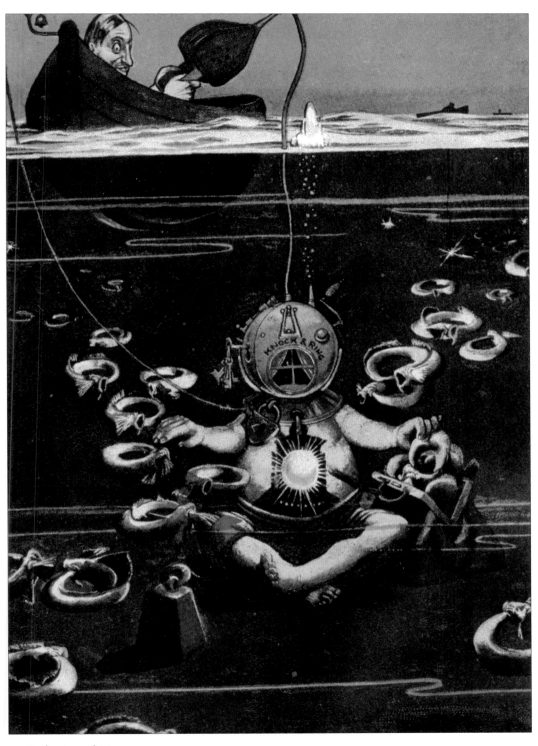

Gathering whiting.

Trapping whelks.

'Grousing' in the valley of the Thames.

How to catch a tiger.

Porpoise sticking.

Gathering edelweiss in the Pyrenees.

A decided catch: the whitebait cycle. An ingenious contraption necessitated by the exorbitant charges for the hire of boats at the seaside this season.

Tarpon fishing de luxe.

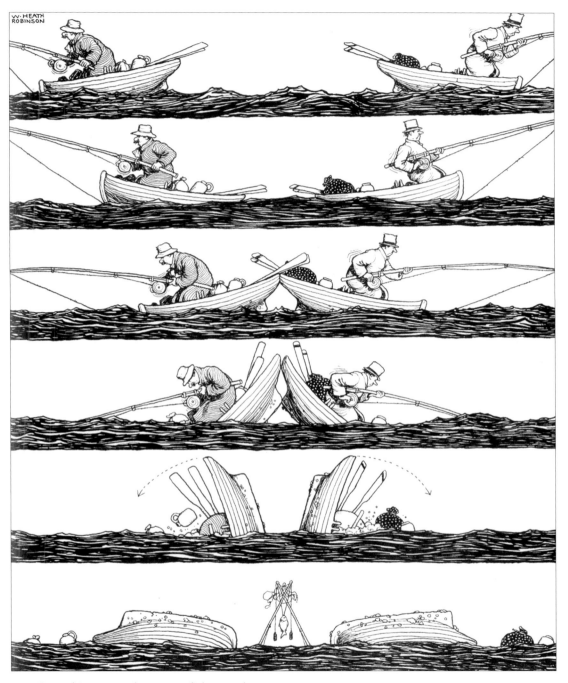

Something on each way – a fish tragedy.

A 'sole'-ful task. Before you go away, a new exercise for encouraging confidence in fishing from an open boat.

Landing an anchovy on the Welsh Harp at Hendon.

The bite. A striking example of how patience is sometimes rewarded in angling circles.

A moving picture. Showing a piscatorial tragedy in one short reel.

The vicious circle. Unsportsmanlike conduct of a trout during the trouting season on Hampstead Ponds.

Also available from Amberley Publishing

HEATH ROBINSON

At Leisure

'I really have a secret satisfaction in being considered rather mad.'

The name of William Heath Robinson has entered the national vocabulary as a by-word for eccentric inventions and makeshift solutions – and with good reason. His world of cogs, bits of string, magnets and precarious tipping points holds a universal appeal.

In this classic collection, Heath Robinson leads a life of leisure, taking a look at some of our favourite pastimes. Seaside holidays, dinner parties with the neighbours and dancing classes are all reimagined and given the Heath Robinson touch in a bid to make them just that little bit easier – whether they needed it or not.

£10 Paperback
96 pages
978-1-4456-4596-4

Available from all good bookshops or to order direct
Please call **01453–847–800**
www.amberley-books.com

Also available from Amberley Publishing

The name of William Heath Robinson has entered the national vocabulary as a by-word for eccentric inventions and makeshift solutions – and with good reason. His world of bits of cogs, bits of string, magnets and precarious tipping points holds a universal appeal.

The world of travel is lampooned and reinvented in this brilliantly funny collection of Heath Robinson cartoons. The railway system, cars, boats and planes are all given the unique Heath Robinson treatment, from cow-catching devices to homemade safety gliders, providing hilarious and impossibly solutions to the travel problems we never even knew existed.

£10 Paperback
96 pages
978-1-4456-4595-7